The School Rule

Story by Annette Smith

Illustrations by Samuel Sakaria

Contents

Chapter 1

The New School

Millie made her way carefully along the path towards her classroom.
Today was her second day at this school.

A few children stopped to watch her.
One little boy stared and pointed.

Millie knew the little boy wasn't trying to be mean, so she stopped and waved to him.

"Hello!" Millie said to the little boy.
"I'm new at this school."

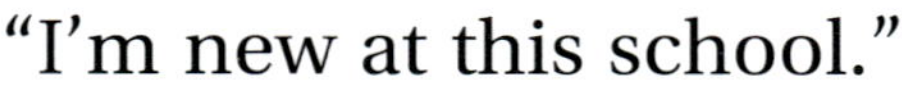

The little boy ran up to Millie and they walked slowly together to her classroom.

Chapter 2

Into the Classroom

"Come on in, Millie," said Ms Jones, with a big smile. "Would you like me to help you with your backpack?"

"No, thank you, Ms Jones," said Millie. "I can reach the peg."

Millie put her backpack on the peg and took out her reading book.

"Millie!" called Laura, from the classroom.
"Come and sit up the front here with us.
You will have to hurry, though.
The bell will be going soon."

Millie nodded and smiled.
"I'll be there as quickly as I can," she said.

But Millie couldn't sit on the mat
with Laura and the other girls.

"Here you are, Millie," Ms Jones said quietly.
"You can sit on this chair.
It can be your turn today
to change the computer screen for me."

"It looks like that new kid is going to be Ms Jones' pet,"
Jake whispered to Ali.

"Shh .... shh ...!" said Ali.

Chapter 3

The Ball Game

At playtime, everyone rushed outside and into the sunshine. They were ready to play their favourite ball game, "Chase the Robber".

But Millie couldn't rush out with them.

"Laura," said Ms Jones.
"Remember to look after Millie.
Please don't leave her alone in the playground."

When Ms Jones had gone over to the office,
Laura and her friends ran to join the others
playing the game.
Soon, they were running everywhere,
as they tried to catch Jake, who had grabbed the ball.

"Look out, Millie!" shouted Jake,
as he raced around the children.
"You're in my way!"

With that, he pushed past Millie and she fell backwards.

At once, some older children came over to help Millie.
"Don't worry. I'm not hurt," she said
to one of the big boys,
who had picked up her crutches.

"I'm glad about that," he said,
"but it shouldn't have happened."

Jake was annoyed that he had been caught.
"That new kid, Millie, has spoilt our game!" he said, throwing the ball to Ali.

One of the big boys, Lucas, heard Jake and went over to him.
"Hi, Jake," he said. "Millie didn't spoil the game. You just weren't quick enough to get out of her way."

“You are right, Lucas,” Jake said,
and he turned to look at Millie,
who was now standing not far away.
“I’m sorry, Millie. I forgot the main rule at our school.”

“What’s the rule, Jake?” asked Millie.

“Look after everyone!” shouted all the children.